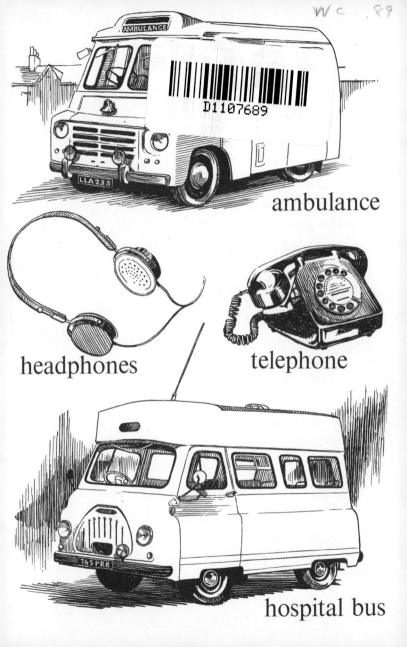

ambulance

headphones

telephone

hospital bus

Series 606B

Here is another carefully planned book which will help to answer the many questions that lively children ask.

Within the limits of a relatively simple vocabulary, interesting and accurate inform-ation is given about life in a modern hospital, and in particular the work of a Nurse.

This book will also help to dispel any fears of the unknown which might be felt by a child about to enter hospital.

'People at Work'
THE NURSE

by VERA SOUTHGATE, M.A., B.Com.
and I. & J. HAVENHAND
with illustrations by JOHN BERRY

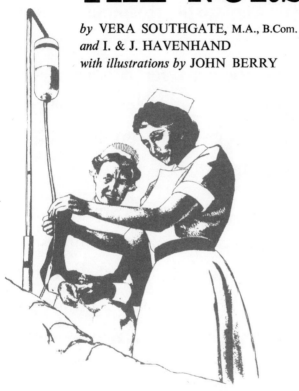

Publishers: Ladybird Books Ltd . Loughborough
© Ladybird Books Ltd (formerly Wills & Hepworth Ltd) 1963
Printed in England

THE NURSE

A nurse's job is to look after people who are ill. Hospitals are full of sick people who need special care to help them to get better. These sick people are called patients. Many nurses work in hospitals, taking care of the patients.

Doctors in the hospitals find out about the patients' illnesses. Then the doctors tell the nurses what to do to help the patients to get better. The nurses carry out the doctors' orders and care for the patients until they are well enough to go home.

7214 0064 7

Patients who stay in hospitals sleep in wards. A ward is a long room with many beds along each side.

Beside each bed there is a locker. This locker has a drawer and a cupboard, in which a patient can keep things.

Sometimes there is a set of headphones behind each bed, so that the patients can listen to the radio when they wish.

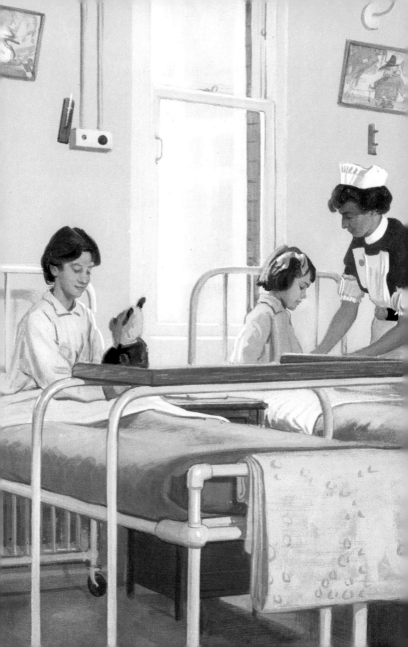

When a patient first comes to hospital, a nurse weighs him and takes his temperature. Then a man in a white coat takes a blood sample from his arm with a needle.

The doctor decides what treatment the patient needs and tells the nurse in charge of the ward how to look after him. She is called the Sister.

When a patient begins to get better he may get up for part of the day. Then he can sit in an armchair or walk about the ward and talk to other patients who are still in bed.

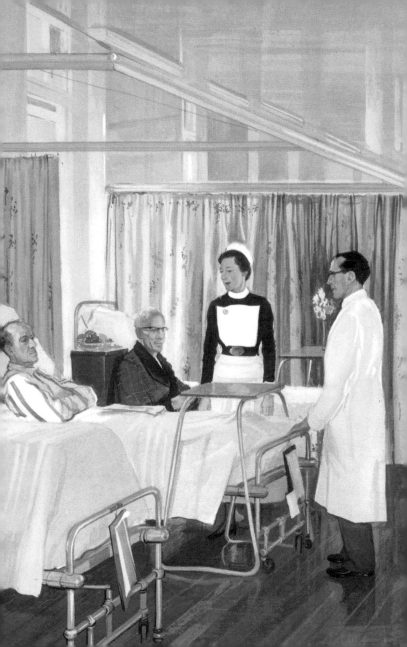

All day and all night, there are nurses in the ward, to look after the patients. It is the Sister's job to see that the patients are given the proper food and medicine, to help them to get well again.

Nurses wear different uniforms in different hospitals. Often they wear blue dresses, white caps and white aprons.

The Sister wears a different uniform from that of a nurse. Usually it is a dark blue dress, a small, white apron and a smaller cap than the nurse wears.

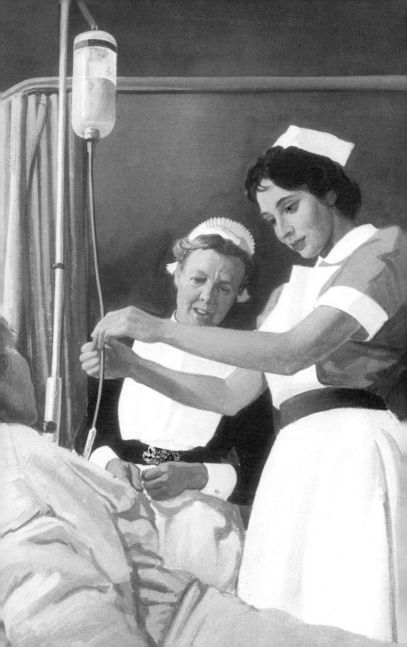

The nurses are always busy. Early in the morning they give the patients cups of tea. Then they help the patients to wash before breakfast.

Most of the patients are given breakfast in bed. After breakfast the beds are made and the wards are cleaned. The nurses give the patients the medicines and tablets which they need.

In hospitals, patients go to sleep very early at night. The last job of the day-nurses is to see that all the patients are ready for sleep.

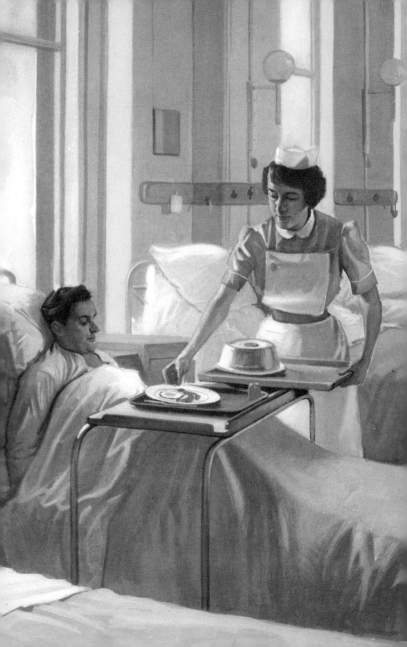

When the day-nurses go off duty, the night-nurse is left in charge.

The night-nurse stays awake all night to look after the patients. She often walks around the ward to see if the patients are asleep. If someone is awake the nurse gives him a drink or anything else he needs.

Sometimes the night-nurse sits at a table, from which she can see all the patients.

Most hospitals have visiting times every day. Then the patients' relatives and friends come to visit them. The patients look forward to the visits very much.

The visitors often bring flowers, fruit, and books for the patients. The visitors sit beside the patients' beds, talk to them and cheer them up. They tell the patients about all the things that are happening at home.

When the visitors have gone, the nurses arrange all the fresh flowers in vases.

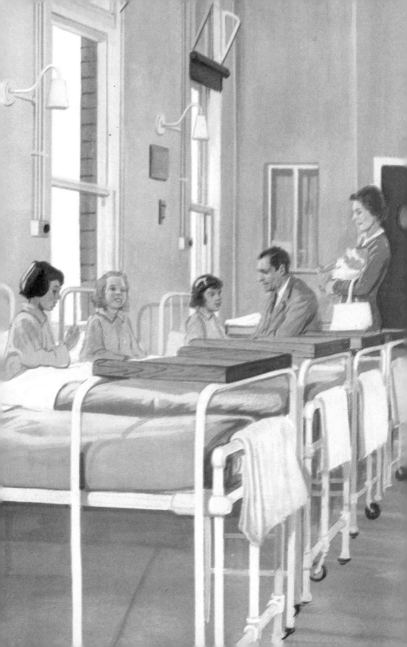

Nurses in hospital work very hard. Although the nurses may sometimes feel tired, they are always cheerful and smiling.

When they are learning to become nurses they have to read books and take examinations.

Many nurses do not live at home. They live together, near the hospital, in large houses called nurses' homes. Each nurse has a room of her own in which she sleeps and reads. There are also large sitting rooms where the nurses can talk to each other and sit and watch television.

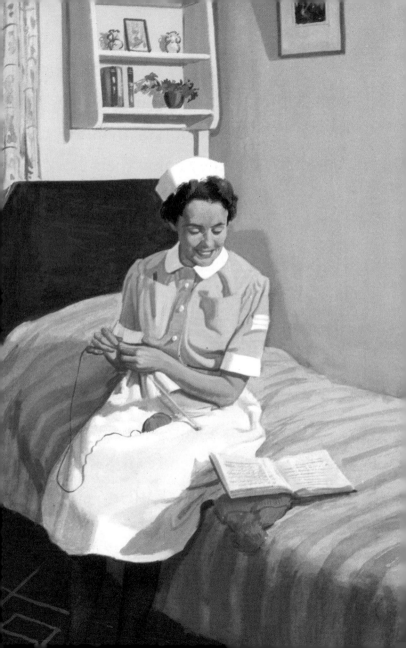

Some wards in hospitals are kept for mothers with new babies. In these wards the nurses are always very busy, but they enjoy their work because they like looking after young babies.

New-born babies need a lot of care. The nurses help the mothers to take care of their babies. The nurses weigh the babies, bath them, and change their clothes.

Everyone is pleased when a new baby is born. Friends often send flowers and cards. Fathers enjoy visiting the hospital to see the mothers and their new babies.

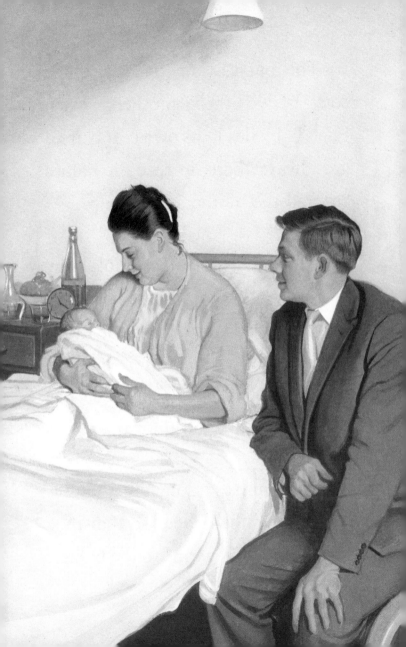

The babies sometimes sleep in cots beside their mothers' beds. Each baby lies in its own cot. Nurses are always there, in case the babies cry and the mothers need help.

All the new babies look very much alike. Nurses make sure that the babies do not get mixed. Every baby has its name on a bracelet round its wrist. The bracelet has letters on it to spell the name.

The nurses sometimes wear masks over their faces so that they cannot pass any germs to the babies.

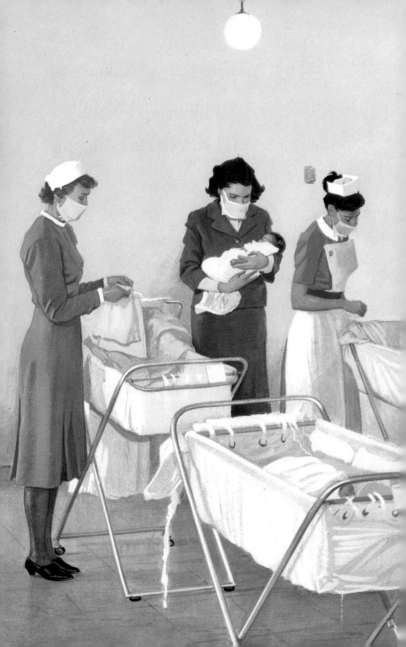

Many patients are taken to hospital by ambulance. An ambulance is a special van to carry people who are ill.

There are stretchers inside the ambulance so that the patients can lie down. Ambulance men can carry a stretcher in and out of the van without disturbing the patient.

The windows of the ambulance are made of special dark glass. People inside the ambulance can see out, but no-one can see in.

Some people are taken to hospital because they have been hurt in accidents. When a person has been badly hurt in an accident, someone can telephone for an ambulance. After a road accident the police often do this.

At all times of the day and night ambulances are ready to take people to hospitals. Many ambulances are fitted with radio telephones. They can then be sent quickly to the places where they are needed.

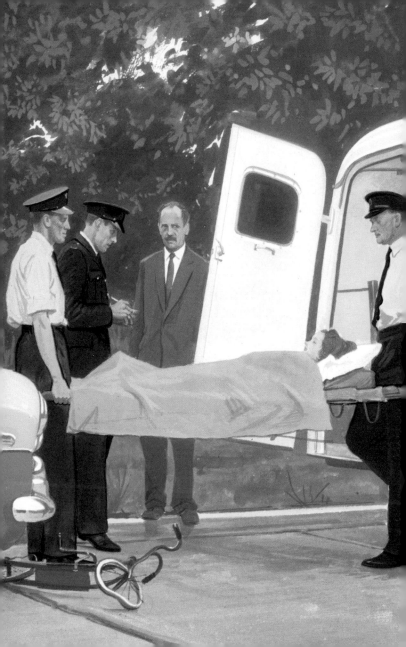

When the ambulance arrives after an accident, the ambulance men lift the injured person on to a stretcher. Then they slide the stretcher gently into the ambulance.

One ambulance man, or a nurse, sits in the van beside the injured person.

The driver then drives to hospital as quickly as he can. He can use his siren or his flashing light to tell other traffic to keep out of the way.

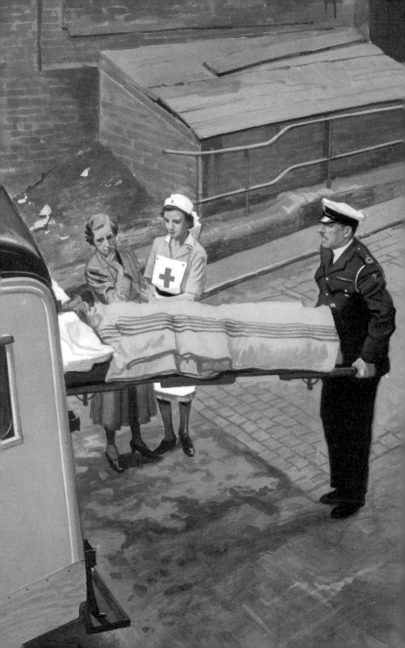

At the hospital the ambulance is driven to the door of the Casualty Department. Here doctors and nurses are always on duty, ready to help people who have had accidents.

If the person is badly hurt the ambulance men carry him into the Casualty Department on a stretcher. If he is only slightly hurt the ambulance men may take him inside in a wheel-chair.

A doctor examines the injured person at once. If he is badly hurt, the doctor will want him to stay in hospital. A nurse will help the patient into bed and look after him.

People do not always go to the Casualty Department by ambulance. If they have had small accidents, they can go to the Casualty Department of a hospital by themselves.

Sometimes accidents happen in the school playground. If a girl falls and hurts her arm or leg she can be sent to the Casualty Department. If the doctor finds that the arm or leg is broken a nurse will help to put it in plaster. The child will then be sent home.

A large hospital usually has a special room called an X-ray room. Here there are X-ray machines which take photographs of people's bones.

When someone has hurt a leg or arm the doctor may want to see an X-ray photograph. The photograph will be developed quickly and the doctor will be able to see if any bone is broken.

An X-ray machine can also be used to take photographs of a person's chest, lungs, stomach or head.

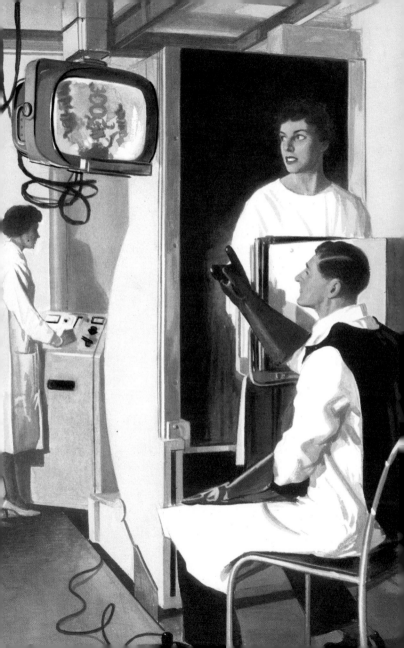

Sometimes a person who is ill needs to have an operation to make him better. Most big hospitals have operating theatres where the doctors do operations. Nurses help the doctors. They all wear masks and very clean gowns.

The patient does not know anything about what happens in the operating theatre. He is given an injection which makes him fall asleep. Then he is put on a trolley and taken to the operating theatre.

When the patient wakes up again, he is in bed in the ward and the operation is over.

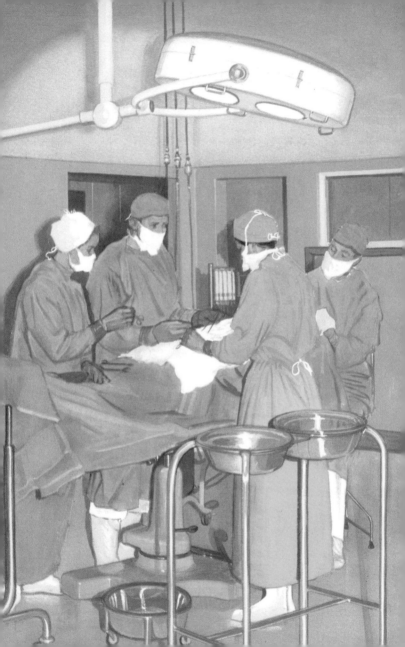

Another department in a hospital is called the Outpatients Department. Some people who are ill do not need to stay in hospital. They can visit the Outpatients Department where doctors and nurses will give them the treatment they need.

Some patients travel to the Outpatients Department of the hospital by themselves. Other patients are not well enough to do this. They can travel on a special little ambulance bus. The bus comes to people's houses to collect them.

Some wards in hospitals are kept for children. Children's wards are happy places. Even though the children are ill, they enjoy staying in hospital until they are better.

Mothers can usually visit their children any time of day. They bath them, dress them and help to feed them. The children are pleased to have their mothers with them. The nurses are glad to see them too, because they keep the children happy.

The food is just the kind which children like. Often there is ice-cream and jelly. The children think it is fun to eat their meals in bed.

When the fathers have finished work in the evening, they come to the hospital to say goodnight to their children.

There are always lots of toys in a children's hospital. Those children who are able to walk about, play games with the children who are in bed.

There are always many interesting story books in the ward. There are picture books for the youngest children and plenty of comics. Sometimes there are big toys such as a doll's house, a rocking horse, or an engine.

When the nurses have finished their work they enjoy playing with the children.

Sometimes a hospital has a teacher who visits the children's ward every day.

The teacher takes lessons with the children who are not in bed. Sometimes all the children have a singing lesson together.

Then the teacher sits beside each child who is in bed and helps him with his reading, writing and sums. She leaves the child some work to do in bed. Next day she marks the work. The children like having lessons to do in bed.

Children who are in hospital at Christmas have a wonderful time.

A week before Christmas the ward is decorated with streamers and balloons. Each ward has a lovely Christmas tree with presents on it.

On Christmas Eve, after the lights are put out, the children are told to listen for the carol-singers. All the nurses walk into the ward, carrying little lamps. Then, they sing Christmas carols for the children.

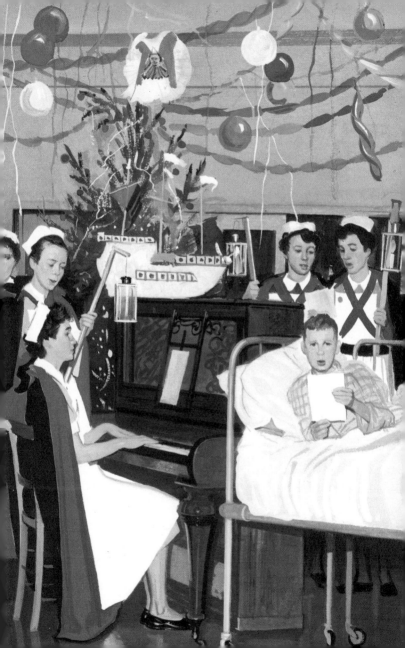

On Christmas morning every child looks in the stocking which is hanging at the end of his bed. All the stockings are full of presents.

The children enjoy a very good Christmas dinner of turkey and Christmas pudding. They eat nuts and fruit. They pull crackers and wear paper hats.

After dinner Father Christmas visits the wards and gives every child a present from the Christmas tree. Christmas in hospital is great fun for children.

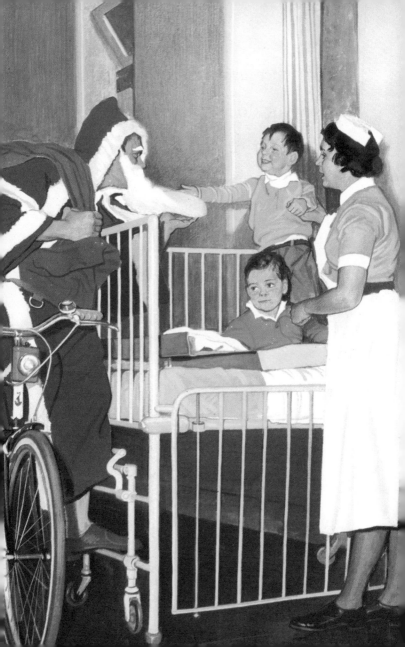

When a child is beginning to get better, the doctor says he can get up for an hour or two every day.

Then when the child is quite well he can go home again. His mother and father take him home. He is pleased to be going home, but sorry to leave his friends in the children's ward.

Mother and father are glad that the doctor and nurses in hospital have made their little boy or girl well again.

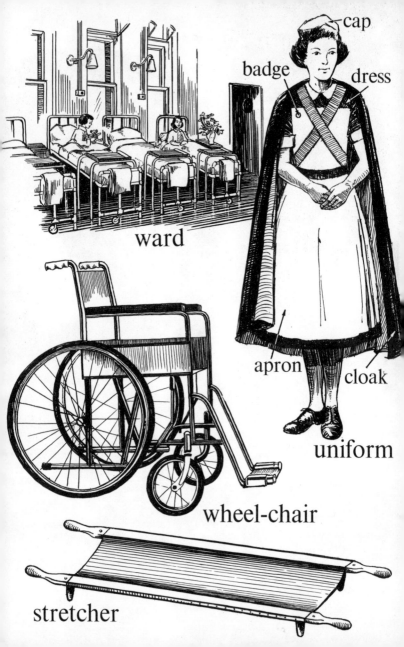

ward

cap

badge

dress

apron

cloak

uniform

wheel-chair

stretcher